NEW YORK CITY
3rd Avenue Loves

By EMMANUEL LATOUCHE

PAROLE DES HOMMES
PEACE IN THE WORLD
WITH YOU! POEMS—1990
AMERICA MY LOVE
HAITI, I LOVE YOU
LA VIE DES PAUVRES
COMPLICATIONS
169 LESSONS OF LOVE

NEW YORK CITY
3rd Avenue Loves

Emmanuel LaTouche

To order additional copies of this book, contact:
Xlibris
844-714-8691
www.Xlibris.com
Orders@Xlibris.com
832234

Contents

NEW YORK CITY 3RD AVENUE LOVES
THIS BOOK, YOU ARE NOT BELIEVE YOU COULD
PUTTING BACK WITHOUT TO LOVES IT.
USUALLY, PEOPLE STOPPING ON THE DIAMONDS
WITHOUT TO MENTIONED THIS IS A DIAMONDS.
JUST ENJOYS THE POETRY.
TOMORROW WILL BE ABLE TO HELP YOU IN LOVES.

Ultimate Loves

Why so long for my last kisses
Why at the last goodbye you remember me loves
Why at the times I cannot stand up you love me
Why? Why? For my last words
Each one of you thinking about me
II
Please! Do not wait for my eyes to close any day
To loves me, just telling me now!
Please! Do not coming in my funeral
To shank hands with others
Please! Let me leave in PEACE
III
I am a survivor for my last words
I am strong for my sickness
I am a fighter for my Diabetes
By any day now! My goodbye not too far
From me, I am strongest for that!
IV
When I gone, I do not want people to crying for me
I love music, just give me some music...
When I gone, I will find my PEACE
No more talking, no more crying for me
I will be fine, for my words!

Did I Missing My Exit Tonight!

No, maybe yes,
May I ask for help
No, I knew my place
What is wrong to me
You said, you are waiting for me
II
I had gas in my car, just for you
I did my hotel reservation for you
I make order for your foods and liquor
You tell me
I loss, did you LOVE me
III
Please! Tell me more, you LOVE me
Longtime, I am waiting for your LOVE
Today Yes, do not make me
Suffer for your cake, I need help
Your face, telling me another LOVE
IV
Baby, why? Why?
You have, this on you tonight
Tonight, is a night
My Hennessy cannot wait any mores
I want all your LOVES, just give it to me!

Are You Still Loves Me!

Please, do not hurt me
Like that! I LOVE YOU
Do you remember me
For the time
You are shoot me
II
Please, tell me
You LOVE me, like I do love you
The raining day, we were at the Disco
The S.O.B. place, dancing Disco all nights
Many people were Eyes Witnesses our LOVES
III
Why today, were so sad for us to be in LOVES
Just tell me... You Love me
Tell me now! If you change me for others LOVES
I feel to go back, but! Too far away for LOVES
Listen my heart still Beep, beep for you
IV
Many peoples looking around to find one like me
Why, why you should remember me?
Somedays, in your life, my pictures will be in you
From places to others without imaginations, LOVES
No matters what, I cannot forget you!

Loves And Beauty

Do not stopping your car,
To said Hello! To a beautiful lady
To thinking she is already love you
She is not yet, in love with you
Loves, that is a magics words to built

II

Not to be playing in the Broadway Show tomorrow
Loves is Special with all meanings to built
Not for you, to playing games in your car
Understood the Power of LOVES
Even you are a Master of LOVES

III

Women had a PHD, for LOVES
Never and ever told a lady
You love her, without to prove her tomorrow
Remember, tomorrow never come
Without a date, just setup yours, if not already

IV

Always showing her, many things in appreciation
A simple thing in life, could make you in motion
Tomorrow, another day to become
For a new life... Respect for each other
Loves and Beauty Forever!

Why She Said That To Me...

Why She told me, She Lose it
Why... Do I should believe it
I do not need to know what was wrong to you
To lets people knowing you lose it
That is your problems it is not my problems
II
Just remember keep your problems
Inside of you...
No one needs to know your own problems
When, two or three peoples knowing you
You are coming a street talking as a lose it
III
Why? You are telling that
At Seventeenth years old you lose it
Why? My mother used to say that is my DIAMOND
Today, I do not have it
I do not know the way to find it
IV
Any day someone like you, will find another DIAMOND
You cannot have it back, too many people love it
All the time people repeat the DIAMOND
Is forever, why... You Lose it?
Too many young men running after me for that!

V

Most of them, want a piece of me
They want to touch me
To playing with me
To teaching me LOVES for that
What did you said, please go slow for me!

Collections Underwear

What a feeling for a young man
Go doing Laundry, just to stoking the lady underwear
All times, he going to work with lady underwear
For what reason, he did that!
The nickname, lady underwear
II
The sick man, had a dream to find a lovely woman
When he stolen the lady underwear, he smiles it
Save it, and his pocket sometimes
He sings songs with it, like a Cowboy man
He loves many colors underwear
III
The neighborhood very scares, they are not talking
About it, their loses underwear
Many friends talking with him to be a good man
He is never hear to no one, than a lovely woman
He believes He should have this woman
IV
The one, he loves so much the underwear
The red one, that is favorite colors
Sometimes, he wants to talk about it
He is very scares for people do not put him out
No games in LOVES, he is underwear man

V

Making him crazy to looking for one to sleep tonight
He is talking about it all days
The lady next door, do not go at the same
Laundry anymore, just for him, crazy man
He talks too much about February fourteenth

VI

He does not have a specific girlfriend to talks
Act like a crazy for women,
Many surprising outside he when in the bar
For a great date, with this woman
The lady next door, coming for underwear man!

Listen, Listen Inside...

Never turn your back from your dreams
Is yours, that is the way to survive
Never say you cannot do it! Try anyway
You should do it you keep going
You should make it work!

II

Life is so beautiful if you practice
The self-esteem and listen others
Never again think twice to answer yes!
Go anywhere from your imagination
And practice... Practice to listen!

III

Practice... To do anything you want!
Use your imagination to work for you
Be a creative person, never say you cannot
The future is yours, nobody else, only you
Remember for yourself... Yourself... You

IV

You are today the man tomorrow
You are today the woman tomorrow
Keep practice every time in your life
Keep going anyway you want to go...
Keep listen, listen the self-esteem!

Just Telling Me, Again...

Telling me again, you love me
Like before, you are never love me
Please, continue to open your heart for me
You are everything for me
Just telling me, again...

II

Day after days, I am waiting for you
Every step I did your pictures staying in my heart
I have feeling you are there with me
Please, continue to love me
I cannot give up your LOVE

III

I have always feeling happy for you
You change my heart
This color so beautiful inside on me
Please, coming to enjoys this one with you
My color cannot change, telling me, again...

IV

Another day, for my notebook of LOVE
Another day, together again, for the real LOVE
I have feeling you are kissing me
Just touching my feet, and my heart already open for you
The engine start for your love!

Unhappy Child

Why is the world turning back on us?
Why no one cannot come to help us?
Why no one does not even ask for us?
Please! Saying something about us
Turning your eyes on us
II
Today, many of us do not have a mother
Tomorrow will be a charm for us, without a mother
Please! Saying some words for us
Come for us, Coronavirus pandemics finish us
What a live, living on the streets without a mother
III
Yesterday, we were born by a mother
Today growing up on the streets lonely
Be a child without a mother, lonely
Tomorrow, the Mother's Day for us
But! A child without a mother living lonely
IV
Became an unhappy child, in this beautiful world
People with great heart survive us
Five cents to a dollar, make different in life for us
What a life, without parents in this world
Should every child without parents suffer like US!

V

Mother, why you not there for us
Why no one cannot come for us, we are lonely
The rain, sun, snow, and many catastrophes for us
Your present, very necessary, no home, no foods for us
You were a best parent we are still love YOU!

Please! Tell Us

Tell us, what is going on
We want to know about the world
Too many of us, cannot talks
Our breathe, stopped tell us
Coronavirus pandemics...What is going on
II
We deserve an answer, too many of us
Cannot even talking about it in this world
No more news for us, Coronavirus kills us
The Coronavirus pandemics coming for us
No one knows what is going on
III
Many of us, do not have hopes any mores
Hospitals no more places for us
On the Streets no more Masks
The hand Sanitizers too expensive
To buying store closes, we need foods
IV
What is going on, landlords do not like us
Tomorrow will be betters. Yes! They have hopes
For how long-term, should we insides
Many months comings and no foods for us
Please, do not judges us

V

We are humans, we are born to survives
Helping us, to find the ways to get hopes
Many peoples gone, the one without names
The funeral homes cannot accepter any mores
Believes it, the world tomorrow will be betters

VI

Do not crying brothers and sisters
The rules of life, in three words
One, you are born with happy faces
Second, you must be living in this world
Third, the times to go without regrets!

One Of Us Gone!

Why, it is a time for Him to gone
Why, like that!
Please, tell us what is going on!
Eight minutes and forty-six seconds his gone!
For what, his gone!

II

Please, we are not dogs, why like that!
Talks to us, what is going on!
The world today, does not function like before
Many of us crying daily for our children's
One of us Gone!

III

The world very solidarities for Him
George Floyd, still alive
Too many of us gone
Without answers, just told your children's
The rules of lives

IV

United States of America, crying for you
Every corner in every city, cannot stop crying
Who is next, too early to like that!
Around the world, no words cannot come out
From many of us, we have a mission for our children's

V

The tears of my eyes, cannot stop
Why, so many of us, crying for Him
He was a live, without enemies
He is gone for answers the world rules
Just remember the price for our colors

VI

Even, they are talking you, you must be careful
Coronavirus pandemics finished us like that!
Many, many of us crying without stops
May 25th, 2020, this is another day to remembered
People losing everything, they have in the businesses

VII

People breaking up doors and stilling everything
Fires everywhere, even the POLICE STATIONS burn down
POLICE CARS etc., What is going on!
Talks to us, why?
Why, PEACE cannot be done in this planet?

Nonconforteble Candidate

Very Big mouth talking trash daily
He wants to be president for a group of people
Should the world be happy for Him!
Money cannot buy power for a candidate
Be a president you must love each other
II
Talking trash daily cannot go... No way
Talking like a dreamer for some people
Money cannot make you president for other
Living with gold and broken daily...
This is not yours
III
Go back thinking about daily words
Cursing people, angry about other
Cannot go in the White House
Educations it is a key to success
Love yourself before you love somebody
IV
Remember RNC are a great Institutions for others
Not for people like you to be there
Cursing people daily expend money for people
Enjoys the material things not a success
Understanding life before the White House!

I Said No...

No means no, no to be down for my life
A great fighter, always believe for life
To be a better man tomorrow
Please! Tell me, the rules for tomorrow
I have a fight, again and again for my life
II
No one, wants to tell me anything
Tomorrow will be better for my fighting
Just tell me, I am ready for tomorrow
When tomorrow coming, many of us will be happy
Just to be in my corner unhappy
III
I learn from my mistake daily, just to stand up happy
Sun, rain, snow, and cold times, I am
here to make you happy
I never and ever be a sad man, I have happy face
That is the one I am living daily, just my face
If you like it or not, I am me...
IV
No one cannot be like me
Love me or leave me
I have a mountain to catch up soon
No one, wants to go with me
Tomorrow at the same time, noon!

My Fight Tonight

I lost my gloves, I will be late for my fight
People waiting for me, no one known tonight
What a superb future fight
One of us going down
Peoples beginnings in
II
Lots of commentaries both sides
Peoples births on me or the other
I do not have enough people for me
But! I believe in myself for tonight
I saw my old friend for a long date
III
Him and is family come to supporting me
Not enough times to talking
We will be able to talk after the game
Five minutes after, times for the rings
I have five guys on my corner
IV
The show down in Madison Square Garden
Peoples still crossing the Streets on every corners
No one known who is going to be the winner
The confidents on each either way
One of us will be a winner today!

Accidents At 14ᵀʰ Street

The Yellows cab, and an Ambulance
The Cab driver going up on Third Avenue
The Ambulance driver crossing 14ᵗʰ Street
The Ambulance horns sound everywhere on the Street
Maybe the Cab driver not putting attentions
II
Peoples. Always want to be the eyes-witnesses
One, to two minutes many peoples
Outside of the Streets, each one asking questions
What is going on?
Nobody dead, yes or not
III
Some peoples talking, it is not a big accident
Thanks God!!!
Only the Cab crashing on the driver sides
No passengers inside the Yellow Cab
For the Ambulance, nobody hurts
IV
You know why... The accident not too big
Because, it is Sunday, not too many peoples
On the Streets in New York City
The streets are half empty, not afternoon yet
God always great for all of us!

Should I Believe
On My Age!

Why the times going too fast
Why, not any more 24 hours a day's
Why, it is only 8 days a week people workings
Many peoples crying for long days workings
Without salaries, only the bosses could survive
II
Years ago, growing up in the Island of Haiti
It was Pearl Des Antilles
Music, Beauties artisanal, Markets all was for Haiti
What is happen today, the world forgets us
Even some progress, without success
III
Growing up on the Island of Haiti
Many souvenirs without data, for some of us
Still built up the documentaries
If one day, one of us will be able to remember
The beauties of Haiti
IV
Why peoples, killings others for power
Why politicians are the same corruptions brains
They are users the poor peoples for the owns beneficiary
Give them, moneys, alcohols, foods etc.
Tomorrows, there are not be the same anymore

V

All are the same peoples, want to be a dictator
Politicians corrupts the world with moneys
Even the one the best educates peoples
They are working like dogs for them
Why the times going so fast, not anymore 24 hours a day

VI

Only 8 days a week, the emptying farms without peoples
In the stores, people take care yourselves
No more patrons to serves you, serve yourselves
Day after days, technologies changing the world
Tomorrow, educations will be online only!

VII

The world moving too fast for the one who late
Must be ready for the technologies
Just remember, 8 days a week very sooner
Everything must move faster,
Too slowly, cannot have the success of life

VIII

Why, my colors it is my mistakes
I am feeling, I am a human being
My brain is powerful with LOVES
Why my colors want to kill me
Some of them still loves me

IX

Maybe, I am too old for them
But not too much to accept me
For whomever remember me
One day's my words will be great for them
When American peoples, unified togethers

X

The lights of Glorified the world
Shall be comings for us
When each one of us, forget about discriminations
BLACK LIVES MATTER, united for same causes
PEACE will be able working in AMERICA!

Unforgettable Kisses

Two great friends living in the neighborhood
One had a family of six persons
The others had three persons
Doors to doors with different numbers
Family of six have a difficulty for their children

II

The biggest problems arrived at night times
For those children to find a place to sleeps
The children are 16, 14, 10, and 7 years old...
They are living in the two bedrooms apartment
The lives coming difficult for them

III

The family of three have a greatly lives styles
Father, mother and a little son of 4 years old
Living in the gorgeous house of fourth bedrooms
And the superb three bathrooms
Very easily live.

IV

The father of six looking for a job
For his sixteenth years old son
One day, it was stopping by his neighbor
And begin to talk about his problems
For his son, looking for job

V

Because his son in the high school now!
He must have been looking for job
The home they are living coming to small for them
Six persons in two bedrooms apartment
The conditions of live

VI

Not too great for them
The neighbor of three proposal an idea to him
The gentleman told him
His is going to talk to her wife for him
What they are going to helping him

VII

The wife from neighbor accepting the idea of him
She told the husband, give the young man a room
In the basement to live for some time
With that he could be able to look for job
With a contentment to be in home not too far

VIII

The father of six, when back home
To talk with his family about it
The way, his neighbor had a great heart
To open the doors for his son
The son found a job in the Super Market

IX

Not too far, from the place it is living
Half a miles, distance from the house
After school, he stays on his job for three or four hours
Weekdays, in the weekend it is working more hours
After two weeks working, he when upstairs

X

To talk with owner wife to know how much
The basement room, the woman answered him it is free
To living here, still you are going in the college
He thankfully them for the help
The husband of three, working as a truck driver

XI

DELIVERY GAS FOR SHELL, it is always on the roads
Sometimes his working a week straight
To makes moneys, sometimes five days
Usually, he came late at nights find everyone sleeping
Many Time the wife running downstairs to check-in

XII

On the young guy if he already in
Sometimes, she gives the guy foods
One night, he was studies for the school home works
And she come down to delivery foods to him
And find the young man playing games

XIII

OF LOVES, lots of kisses, one after one
They are starting to date for sometimes
Now! Do not suffers any mores for LOVES
Even the young man went in Colleges
She is in still in LOVES with Him!

One Our Leader Is Goner...

The combats do not stop us
He did it in 1960th, the flames still alive for 2020th
Someone else keep the flag for us
We have a mission to promise lands
No one cannot stop us.

II

George Floyd, not there anymore for us
John Lewis, leaving us
For this, The Congress missing one
We still looking for someone to carries the flag for us
Just we are looking for you, helping us

III

The roads never too long for us
We are waiting to cross this Bridge for 2020th
In Portland, Oregon peoples are suffering for justice
Soon, many other peoples should be crying in this land
Why, the injustice cannot be in the promise lands

IV

Children, parents crying daily without stop for justice
Even the Coronavirus pandemics eating us
Without stops, no one known for how long-term with us
Inside the hospitals no beds, no supplies for peoples
Please, saying a word for them, politics always there

V

Loves one, cannot be back
Our souls in this land survives
The memories not forgotten
Why, they are fighting for power
Seat down, thinking who are going to suffers

VI

The names are AMERICANS, not other nations
Other nations will be enjoying for demagogies
We will lose our Titles number One
For now! Americans do not have respect in our land
We must be wake up in looking back Americans!

Why Lady Liberty Crying?

Why, too many peoples crying today?
Why, AMERICA the world closed doors on you today?
Why, peoples from this beautiful country crying today?
Brothers do not like the other brothers
Sisters do not like other sisters
II
AMERICA, your reputations like a game to survives
Even your children cannot survive any mores
What is going on, Lady Liberty Crying today
Please, tell me what is going on in this country today
Why, so many peoples crying everywhere today
III
What is going on, AMERICA, no more tears
Many friends told me no more tears
Some do not have foods for a day
The others, forget about them only themselves
Why, the divisions in this land, just for one only!
IV
The color of skins kills so many of us
Before you are going on the streets, they do not like us
The one on power, forget about us
The Coronavirus pandemics coming for us
We are still crying for you Lady Liberty!

Freedom For Us!

We want it, we are suffered too much for it
Longtime ago, theirs used us
Without stops, it is a time for us
That is your right, stand up for right, used it
FREEDOM FOR US!
It is the times for us, just wake up, wake up
Tomorrow will be better if we are
Together and wake up, wake up
The times is right here, VOTE, VOTE
FREEDOM FOR US!
Just tell me my color, I am FREE
I am a Voter, I know my rights to VOTE
Times to choose the right or the left,
Used your FREEDOM, VOTE, VOTE
FREEDOM FOR US!
Stand up, someone else will be able to help you do it.
VOTE, VOTE... No one cannot buy your FREEDOM
You are born to be FREE, use it, enjoys it
No one cannot take it away from us!

Why You Hates Someone?

Just telling me why?
Why you have too many enemies
Just telling me your problem with others
Why you turned back to something great for the world
Just telling me your problem with others
II
Lets talking about the others
Lets talking about opening your hearts for others
Do not judge other people with hate
All born to survive, with different lusts
Judge yourself before someone else
III
Do not say you are okay
Do not put everyone in your shoes
Give them respect to have respect for others
The lives are too tight for your grandeur
Are you thinking, you charge of the world!
IV
Just imagine, are quite the life exists
Everything staying in this place, no one cannot take it away
You are coming for your time and living
after your time ready to go to, just enjoys it!
Be peaceful humans being and survival the world!

Do Not Tell Me, How Many Day

Just tell me, your time is up, today
No more talking, just prove yourself today,
Many years ago, you are critical of me
You are the winner, for every corner for me,
Please tell me, who you are today

II

You said you are everything, a master to me.
Just tell me your name,
People calling you a con, without words,
You must learn the way, to love others
Do not be too greedy for money,

III

Any territory, people very scared of you
No one achieves nothing for you
Your words, putting you can perform you as a clown
You are scared others,
You have freedom of speech, say your words,

IV

You can see the world as your backyards
Education, expensive for people without a purpose
Live your life, like an empty brain
Tomorrow will be a glamour time,
You are belonging to the instruction oscillation!

The People View!

I say what I mean, I mean what I say
Just follow me, for what I say
When I stand up, I have better look than I seat down
I am not a clown
Do not judge me

II

I have a name
Do not put me down
I work hard for my salary, pay me
I mean much of my time
To working for you, just follow me

III

You better have a type of recorder
To know me better
Sometimes, I only spoke one time
Because my brain full of words
For twenty more books, just pay me

IV

The little clown no more words
I survive, because of you
Every day I think about you,
No one does not know who loves our faces
We are living with the enemies daily

V

Please, say what you want to say, we are alive
Does not matters you love us or not, daily
The history still alive
Our planet cannot change daily
You are going to loves our faces!

Why You Are, Never Stop Crying?

Everyone has a duration, in life
A time, to be happy with others
A time to be contemplated in life
When your moments coming do not cry for others
A time to laugh at others
II
When your time is reaching
Do not be selfish in life
Just remember you are not for the life
Do not push people who arriving
From other places, that is life
III
You are here because people like you
You do not belong permanently
Everyone likes you, cannot accept you
You must go to a place permanently
You are desirable for others
IV
People crying day-to-day just to know you
Who you are no one recognizes You!
What your formation you are in life
Please, tell us about yourself in life
Talk about your family background in life

V

People want to know you better
Even my pens out of ink today,
I want you to talk to others
Be the best you could in life
Do not regret your mistakes in life

VI

We are humans, all of us doing mistakes daily
Today, it is not your days
You are to accept when your time coming
No one is permanent, that is job today
Tomorrow, someone else will be doing it!

Why Covid-19?

Why? Please tell me why?
Why? They are coming for us, why?
Why? The government knew, no one talks
Why? Forget about us, talks
Please, we are humans like others

II

No tears in my eyes, any more like others
Many brothers and sisters were gone
No one does not care about us, talks
That is sure, we are not from them, talks
The virus coming for us, talks

III

We do not know if we are limited to others
No one remembers us anymore, talks
Saying anything you want, we are one...
Do not forget our roots in Africa, talks
Talks like the others

IV

Saying loud our names, they do not want us anymore
The Covid-19, not built for us only, talks
Should we believe in the Vaccines tomorrow, talks!
We will have it too, perhaps no more
We have the traditional way to survive, talks!

The New Era Is Coming!

Peoples Very Happy, for no parfait ideas
The twenty-twenty, too many sadly memories
All kinds age peoples not survivals the time
Even inside the hospitals, no more places
Many of us cannot stops crying daily
II
What a year, who knows... No one
People greedy for anything this time
Almost everyone known someone
Were gone by this Virus daily
Who could be able to stops the time?
III
The one who like it, or the one still riches
On it, the countries with lots technologies
Benefices on the poor one
The Virus ravages the world economies
People living with sadly memories
IV
The days should be come for the new faces
Peoples waiting too long for the change of power
Brothers and sisters out of the places
They are hungry for anything to buying
No foods, no houses, more bills this time

V

People counting days for liberations
When the new year and the Vaccines
People will have hopes for liberations
The world will be able to have Vaccines
What will happen to the poor countries?

VI

Many of them do not have scientific peoples
Just to find help, UN forget about them nations!
The billionaires do not care for others
The world used moneys for marketing daily
Thanks, the new ERA is coming!

This Right Permitted!

You deserve it, people VOTES for you
You are a winner
Your right is here, enjoys
No one cannot take it away from you
That is the Constitution, you are a winner.

II

Peoples on the Streets to celebrates
You are a winner, enjoys
Discriminations kills many of us
They are calling us names
The Right Permitted!

III

We are waiting too long for you
The 3rd Avenue too many LOVES
People crying so much for you
The Universal Power of LOVES
Still existed, no problems enjoy!

IV

People VOTES for You, JOE BIDEN
Young and adults knows your names
Peoples are cool just for you KAMALA HARRIS!
You are a winner, the door is opening
The times is comings big for us to Celebrates!

Republicans Party!

I used to like them since Ronald Reagan
For me was the best institutions for the young peoples
Now! Day by days peoples changed for better party
What is going on, no one saying anything for better peoples
The institutions for sales, like apartments in Fifth Avenue

II

What is going on, I changed for Independent party
I do not feel to be a Republican any mores
Pleases, tell me what is going on in Americans Politics
No more trust in republicans Party
Everything for sales

III

Why moneys changing the world of politician peoples
Too many peoples greedy for dollars bills
Tell me if you could reverse the winner for looser
Tell me if another country could be trusting USA any mores
USA used to be an International Guards for the world

IV

What is happening todays, no one
cannot trust USA any mores
Why dogs eating dogs for dollars bills in this world
Everyone want to be a Billionaires
Without knowledgebase, and simplicities
Loves yourselves before others

V

Get busies for tomorrow betters party
Do not be too angry about others
The Republicans Party not for sales
Be strong and go homes
America still can be number one LOVES!

The Woman Of Courages!

The Coronavirus Pandemics does not make her scared
The rains, snow, cools times She is answered
The beeper to saves other people lives
She is a believer for the human lives,
At the hospital, she is mostly happy

II

The smiling face, never and ever without LOVES
Beautiful face, people at beds in the hospital happy
The one who Very Sick, she gives them hopes
Always did the conversations with others, lots of hopes
The Coronavirus, it is not a Games!

III

Many Doctors, Nurses, and workers went, without returned
The families crying so hardly, but! That is lives
People come and people gone without a Words
The one in charges does not cares for them Words
Many others making comments without answers

IV

What a live, some pass away, the families not unformed
No friends no families cannot notices about it
The last door no exit any mores
Some people still looking for answers
Better for the love one to staying home sick

V

Many people sick do not want to go to the hospitals
What a love lives, people do not kiss any mores
People do not shank hands any mores
Everyone wears a mask on the Streets
For how long-term, no one know

VI

She is still doing Her Duty, without complaints
She is a lovely a sweet woman, with lots of dignity
The rewards for her, is giving service to others
The Woman of Courage never stop give hopes
LOVES is perseverance to find success tomorrow!

Just for one of many friends, working at the hospitals

Help Me To Know You Better!

Many of us, cannot speak anymore
Most of us do not have any businesses
No way of life for us to continue anymore
Why America loses too many businesses
People lose their lives savings, help us
II
We need help, we need help, help us
Why America turning back on us
Too many of us, do not have hope anymore
Why people are suffered so much in this country
America, wake up, wake up for a better country.
III
The world looking after you
America does not put your children away
America does not ignore your place today
People still believe in you
Your power is more powerful than you.
IV
Open your eyes for tomorrow to be better
People waiting for last words tomorrow,
No one talking to us about tomorrow
No one cannot tell me about you
Just stand up America to be better!

Everything For A Time!

A time, to come, and a time to go
Nothing is forever, doing your time and go
Too many people suffer for you
People cannot stop crying for you
The Coronavirus pandemics, killing us for you.

II

Twenty – twenty, you have a name for us
Too many peoples gone, without words for us
Tell others, what is going on this time
Why, why around two million without a talk
You did to us, and continue to do it every time

III

How much we should be paying to talk
Everything too expensive, and no foods for us
The bills cannot even pay this day
The utility bills and rents, forget about it for us
Foods Bank, the lines are six blocks away

IV

We can even stand up anymore, help us
We deserve to survive we are taxpayer help us
What is going on, Coronavirus finishing us
Even, the time, to helping us... Some against us
They are not American like us.

V

What kind of destiny for the young Americans!
Who is in charges of the law for Americans!
A small fraction of Dollars people suffers for it, talk
Tell us now, about the American dreams, talk
Bye, twenty – twenty too much for us

VI

The moment coming for new faces and new hopes for us
The Bible words, stay forever for us
You have, to understand the things biggest than you
Science is not a game of politics for you
Just learning about time to go!

Tomorrow!

Your time is up, you must go
Even no places to accepting you, you must go
Go, at the place you are belongs, go, go
No one does not want you anymore
You are too much, for the others
II
In 3rd Avenue Loves, too many peoples
Crying daily for you, the number going up every day
Peoples dies just for your mistakes, go
Too many of us, paying every day
You know betters, to reverses the power of peoples
III
Tell me who you are, every corner your name coming up
Social Medias, Fox News, CNN, MSNBC only you up
What is going on America, no more reverses of powers, go
Your time is up today, you must go
Peoples losing lots of moneys on you, go
IV
Three Hundred and fifty-Thousands not enough for you
How many mores, please, saying something, go!
The Reporters outsides waiting for you, go
Billions and billions, peoples still do
not have foods for a day
The rents cannot even payers, what a live, America!

Shithole Country Is Here!

Believe it or not, in this situation like that!
This is America, no way I do not believe it!
America, that is the most loving country
Your America, people cannot stop crying for you.
What is going on, the Coup in the Capitol Hill,

II

How your people going to have respect
The one in charge does not respect himself.
Dog eating dogs for dollars bills
Three hundred sixty thousand gone for them is nothing
No one cares about us, America you are not like that!

III

Unfortunately for some enormous save other lives
The government friends coming for a Coup
No way, where is the respect for America.
Believe it, but life continues without respect.
If America could stand up to others.

IV

Please, tells me about tomorrow better.
The new President must put the pants up.
Tell the world was a mistake, not forever
We are going to learning about new lessons in life.
Easy to look at the mistakes, not easy
to learns from the mistakes!

Doing A Crime Is A Criminal!

Sometime the criminal dresses great, with pretty faces
Some thinks as a king, even without knowledges
In lives too many peoples greedy for moneys,
Some coming to double faces for moneys
What a live, for a criminal with pretty faces

II

Some want the family or friends to control the world
They are, believes in transferred things from others
In this world, you must follow the rules of lives
If you are going too fast-forward, remember the lights
You have, Yellow, Green, and Red, you face!

III

Remember twelve months of the years
Three Hundred sixty-five days, one is for you
The others for someone else to put the lights on you
The good Detective working twenty-four hours a day
It is always on your backs, do not too greedy for moneys

IV

In this world, you are not only one
The laws were written for all of us, just listen to it
If you cannot readings the rules of laws, listen to it
Peoples come and people gone forever
The History still alive for you!

New York City 3rd Avenue Loves

WOW... New York City, the engines of the world markets, if you are a New Visitors in New York City, you must take a walk by the Financials districts, lovely areas in New York City. The real 3rd Avenue LOVES starting here, even peoples living here do not recognizes here any mores. Too many beautifully architectural buildings

The biggest engines in the world economics, starting at 9:30 am to 4:00 pm the Wall Street Markets opening

Peoples crazy insides, many peoples trading everything, after a short look insides the trades, must take a walk by the Bowling Green areas, visiting Statue of Liberty, Museums, Stores, lots of things to do here, shopping for yours and your family, great restaurants, Broadway etc.

Do not forget to stop by a streets Marchand for a superb Hot Dogs, with can Coca-Cola. Everyone did it, why not you?

Like that! Exactly you become a New Yorker, no times to playing... You must have a Destinations if you are not a Tourists, no small jobs or big jobs, all about moneys...

You had to paying bills and taken care of yourself and family.

Do not drink alcohols on the streets, and respect yourself, be a human being, understood lives. Bad things going to jails, good things be able to have success.

Do not believe in NO ONE, only yourself... Good mornings and goodbye!

Lightning Source UK Ltd.
Milton Keynes UK
UKHW011120260821
389362UK00016B/491/J